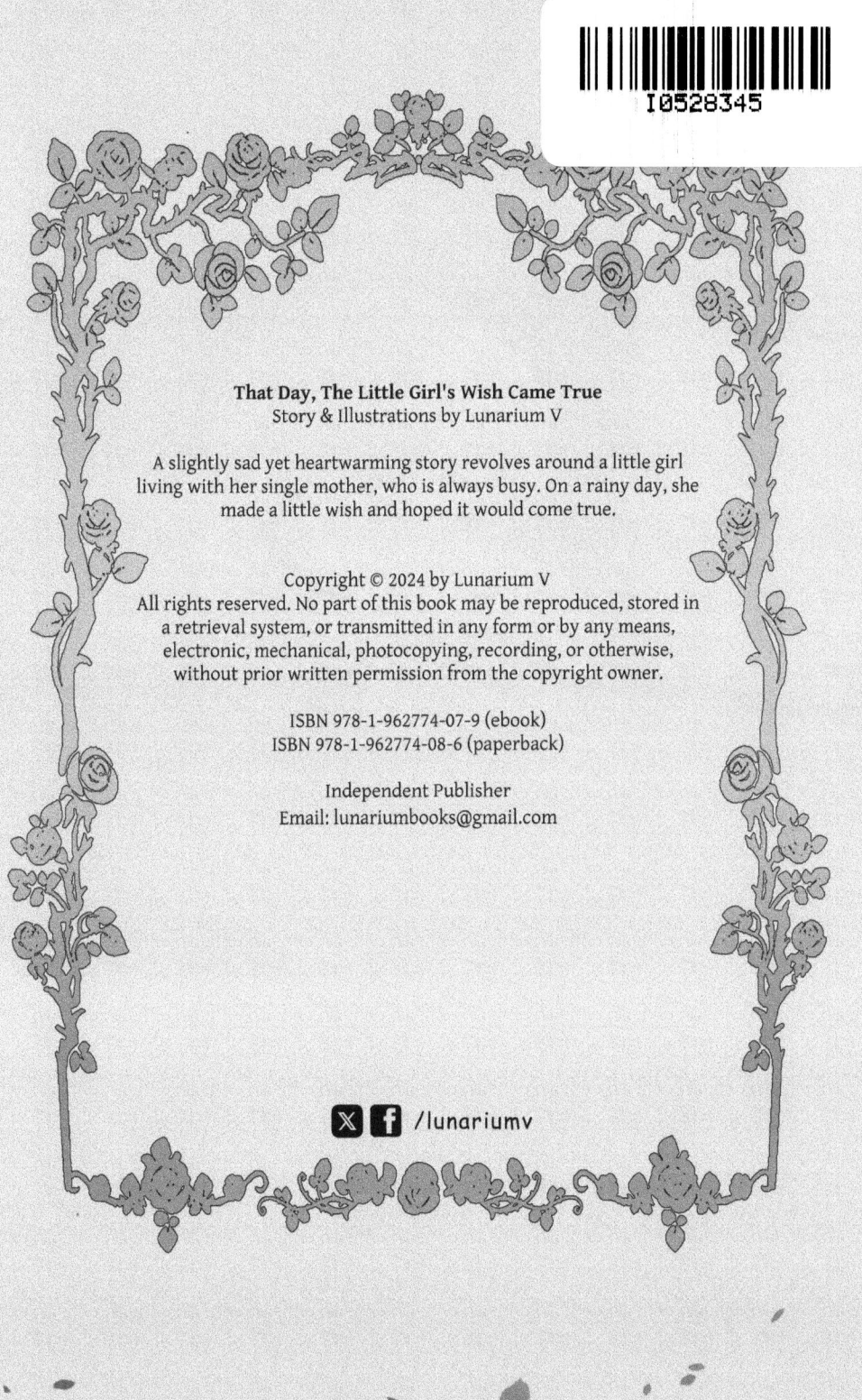

That Day, The Little Girl's Wish Came True
Story & Illustrations by Lunarium V

A slightly sad yet heartwarming story revolves around a little girl living with her single mother, who is always busy. On a rainy day, she made a little wish and hoped it would come true.

ISBN 978-1-962774-07-9 (ebook)
ISBN 978-1-962774-08-6 (paperback)

Independent Publisher
Email: lunariumbooks@gmail.com

𝕏 f /lunariumv

Drip drop, drip drop, raindrops play their song.
Splash, splash, hurried footsteps swiftly throng.

Outside the window, no brilliant shooting star, no
moon, just a somber, raining night.

Gazing at the sky veiled in dark clouds, the little girl
softly murmured. "I hope... I can make new friends."

Tomorrow, the little girl would go to a new school,
but she didn't feel very excited.
It was the third time the little girl had to move with
her mother.

She remembered vaguely the period when they used
to live in a larger, warmer house, perhaps with more
people than this unfamilliar apartment.

Taking slow bites of her dinner, the little girl thought to herself, "Oh, I love my mom's cooking, but it's burning a bit... just like it always does."

Honestly, her mother wasn't adept at culinary skills, often preparing dinner in a rush. In this bustling and costly city, it was really challenging for the young mother to take care of her daughter all alone.

With two regular jobs, including night shifts, and an additional one on weekends at a convenience store, she didn't really have much free time, except for one day off on Sundays. However, almost the only thing she could do was sleep deeply all day, replenishing her energy for the upcoming difficulties.

A morning began...

With a bit of worry about school, the little girl prepared everything in advance. Hair neatly combed, clothes crisply ironed. She arranged each notebook and pencil, carefully placing them in the backpack.

Oh, right! And, of course, before heading out, the little girl would always brighten her day with a cheerful smile in front of the mirror.

Whisper, whisper, the classrooms hum with chatter.

Unfortunately, at school, despite the little girl's longing, her old clothes and shyness couldn't help her make any new friends.

Day after day, she hoped and waited, but her wish... didn't come true.

"I want to have a dad, like everyone else," the little girl thought.

It wasn't the first time she had felt that way, as she witnessed her classmates bragging to each other about how wonderful their fathers were.

At dinner, hesitantly, the little girl asked,
"Mommy... where is my dad?"

And as usual, her mother snapped,
"EAT, YOUR, MEAL!!" Clearly, she didn't even want
to mention it.

The little girl couldn't comprehend it all at such a
young age, somehow, tears... welled up in her eyes.

"Don't cry, I said, JUST STOP CRYING!!" Her mother screamed.
The young mother thought she had enough stress already, working exhaustingly from day to day, bills, and debts to pay... And what could be worse than still having to deal with a child who likes to cry?

Once again, it didn't seem like the little girl's wish could come true.

Snowy, snowy, the fireplace's warmth made all feel cozy.

Today was completely different from every other day. It was Christmas.
Although her mother still had to work the nightshift, luckily, she was allowed to leave early.

The little girl clearly remembered last year when her mother had promised to buy a cute doll for this special night.

Her heart raced with joy, as if all loneliness had gone away. The little girl was really eager to see her mother return home.

She waited and waited for the surprising moment to come.
Finally, her mother arrived home early, but… her hands, shaking from the cold, were empty.
No new doll, no Christmas gift, there was nothing along except the usual tired face, full of impatience.

Glimpsing the last remnants of snow on her mother's hair and clothes, the little girl found herself at a loss for words.

Although very sad, in the tender mind of a child, she still somehow knew that... her mother was just too busy.

"The next birthday, maybe the next birthday I'll get a new doll... Nothing to be sad about," the little girl kept whispering and whispering before eventually falling asleep. "I'll keep being a good girl until then..."

So today, her wish also didn't come true.

Drip drop, drip drop, raindrops play their song.
Splash, splash, hurried footsteps swiftly throng.

Another rainy day, and it seemed to be quite heavy.
The little girl couldn't remember the last time her
mother gently smiled and patted her head... One
year ago, or maybe two years ago? Everything
blurred away with each raindrop on the windowpane.

And this time, the little girl only made a simple little
wish. "I really want to see mom's smile again."

Somehow, the little girl realized that simply waiting wouldn't make anything happen at all.

"Maybe I should do something to make mom happy," she wondered. "Perhaps... a super tasty cake??"

An old, dust-covered cookbook had quietly sat on the shelf for a long time, and at last, it was opened by a tiny hand.

Of course, it was impossible for the little girl to make something so difficult.
She cheered herself up, "Uhm, I watched my mom cooking many times, I... I can do it!"

Eggs, beat it up.
Flour, mix mix well.

Sugar, sweet sweet sweet!!
Salt, hm, a little, just... a little.

Stove, ready on.

...

And after much struggle, syrup and a yummy
strawberry were added for the final touch.

For a first-time chef, the outcome actually wasn't
as pretty as the little girl had expected, though.

Time passed, it was already midnight. And the rain kept falling outside.

Glancing at her petite fingers, still swollen and red from the burn, the little girl murmured, "Ohh, it still hurts... so much..."
But she tried hard to hold back tears, because the little girl remembered that her mother wasn't happy to see her crying.

A familiar sound echoed as the door opened.

Deeds tend to resonate more than mere words. Flour was scattered everywhere, the burnt aroma of cakes mingling with the tempting fragrance of syrup wafted through the air.
After a long minute of being speechless, the young mother understood the situation completely.

Not a single word passed between them, it was unnecessary in this moment. She simply embraced her little daughter tightly, and finally, a weak smile graced the young mother's face.

So today, for the first time, the little girl's wish came true, though together with tears and happiness... amidst a rainy night.

Every child loves their parents, and a mother's love for her children knows no bounds. However, sometimes, love is unspeakable.

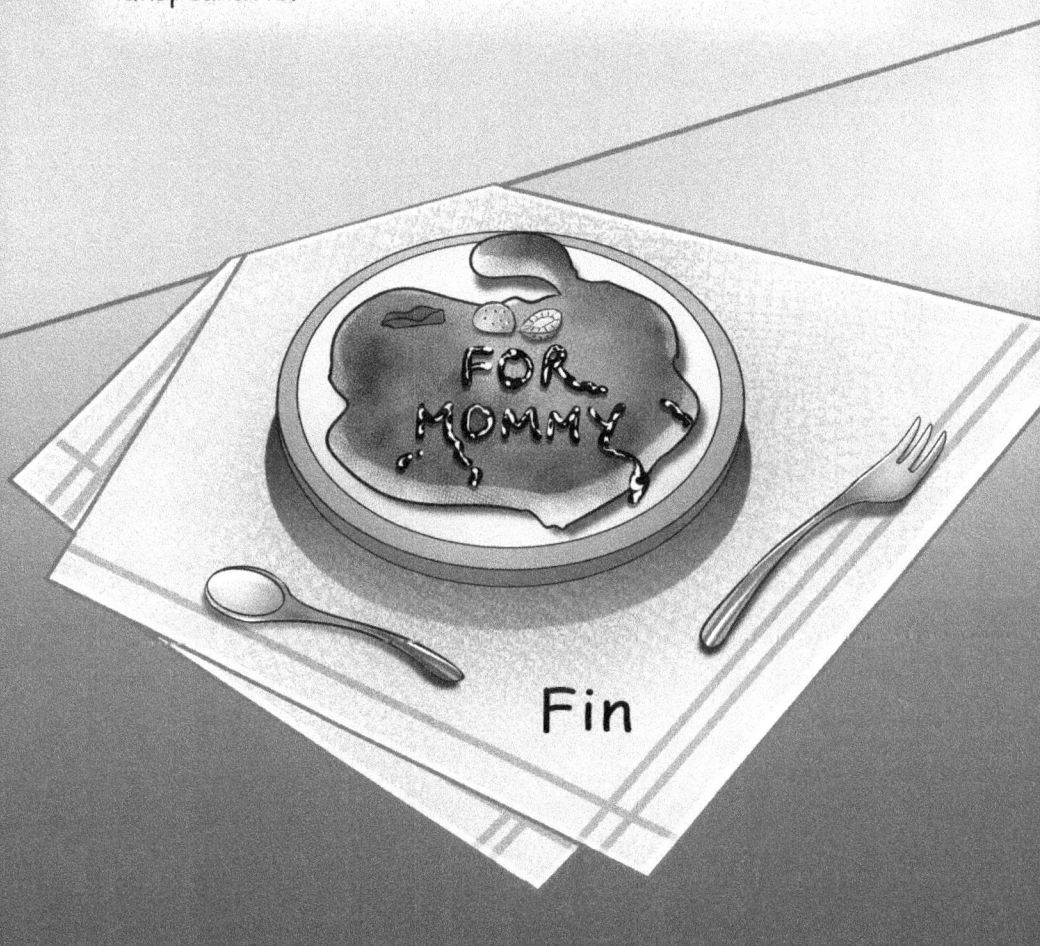

We all have a few embarrassing moments or even painful memories from childhood that we can't forget. It's truly sad if something similar happens to our own children.

Unlike adults, children's souls are delicate and sensitive.

www.ingramcontent.com/pod-product-compliance
Lightning Source LLC
Chambersburg PA
CBHW051253120626
46547CB00014B/1935